THE MEANINGS OF MODERN ART

by JOHN RUSSELL

Art Critic, *The New York Times*

VOLUME **1**
THE SECRET REVOLUTION

THE MUSEUM OF MODERN ART, NEW YORK

I. Edouard Manet
The Folkestone Boat, Boulogne, 1869
Philadelphia Museum of Art

When art is made new, we are made new with it. We have a sense of solidarity with our own time, and of psychic energies shared and redoubled, which is just about the most satisfying thing that life has to offer. "If that is possible," we say to ourselves, "then everything is possible"; a new phase in the history of human awareness has been opened up, just as it was opened up when people first read Dante, or first heard Bach's 48 preludes and fugues, or first learned from *Hamlet* and *King Lear* that the complexities and contradictions of human nature could be spelled out on the stage.

This being so, it is a great exasperation to come face to face with new art and not make anything of it. Stared down by something that we don't like, don't understand and can't believe in, we feel personally affronted, as if our identity as reasonably alert and responsive human beings had been called into question. We ought to be having a good time, and we aren't. More than that, an important part of life is being withheld from us; for if any one thing is certain in this world it is that art is there to help us live, and for no other reason.

It was always so. Art is there to tell us where we are, and it is also there to tell us who we are. It gives pleasure, coincidentally, but primarily it is there to tell the truth. For hundreds of years, and on many matters of supreme importance, it had the edge over all other sources. It gave out the truth about this world and the next one. It encapsulated history. It told us what people wiser than ourselves were thinking. It told the stories that everyone wanted to hear, and it fixed, once and forever, the key moments in our evolution. Art answered the great riddles, filled in the gaps in our general knowledge, and laid Eternity on the line. Above all, it gave reassurance; it told us what we wanted to hear—that experience was not formless and illegible, that man could speak to man without the obstructions of language, and that we were at home in the world, and with one another.

That was long the function of art. Art restored to us the lost wholeness, the sensation of being at one with Nature, and at one with society, which we crave from the moment of birth. Many and desperate are the expedients which we devise for the recapture of that lost wholeness; art restores it completely and forever. So we are quite right to be dismayed when art seems to shift its ground in ways that we find difficult to follow. Still less do we like to think that art might one day peter out. We do not care to echo what was written more than three hundred years ago by Sir Thomas Browne: " 'Tis too late to be ambitious. The great mutations of the world are acted." We should prefer to think— and in my opinion we are quite right to think—that the master-

pieces of our own day can perfectly well stand comparison with the great achievements of the past.

But the anxiety remains. And art *has* shifted its ground, and recoded its messages, and questioned its own nature, and reshaped the ordeal by initiation to which we are subjected before we can understand it completely. Indignation at all this masks feelings to which we dare not give their true name. E. H. Gombrich, with his *The Story of Art,* has taught millions of people how to look at old pictures; and he put this point very well when he said that European Expressionism before 1914 sprang from the fear of "that utter loneliness that would reign if art were to fail and each man remained immured in himself." If the two words "modern art" are enough to start an argument almost anywhere, it is because this fear of the eventual and hypothetical failure of art has come to haunt even people who have never been to a museum, let alone bought a picture.

It was in the second half of the 19th century that art was relieved of certain of the duties which it had been carrying out on society's behalf and became free to look into its own nature. The duties in question had been many and varied. Philip IV never doubted that when his troops won a famous victory his court painter Velázquez (fig. 1) was the best man to commemorate it. When Marat was murdered in his bath in 1793, it was by popular demand, almost, that Jacques Louis David made haste to paint *Marat Assassinated* (fig. 2). When the Houses of Parliament burned down in London in 1834, art gave us our most memorable account of what happened: J. M. W. Turner (fig. 3) was on hand to tell how the great scarf of flame unwound itself high in the night sky. Art had no rival on such occasions. It gave us what we could get nowhere else. Nor was the artist simply a passive recorder: when the French frigate *Méduse* was lost in particularly ghastly circumstances in 1816, it was a painter, Théodore Géricault (fig. 4), who brought the matter out of the newspapers and onto a deeper level of concern.

In paintings such as the ones I have named, people were told what they wanted to know, and told it in a way that allied power to concision and eloquence to understanding. These traits in combination inspired a collective confidence in art. A recent example of that confidence is the first line of a poem by W. H. Auden: "About suffering they were never wrong, the Old Masters." Though not wholly true—some Old Masters were platitudinous and histrionic, others had an attitude toward suffering that was distinctly equivocal—this line does indicate one of the ways in which art helps us to live.

That is to say that we have a deeper understanding of old age

3

1. Diego Rodriguez de Silva Velázquez
The Surrender of Breda, 1634–35
Museo Nacional del Prado, Madrid

2. Jacques Louis David
Marat Assassinated, 1793
Musées Royaux des Beaux-Arts de Belgique, Brussels

3. J. M. W. Turner
Burning of the Houses of Parliament, 1834
The Cleveland Museum of Art

4. Théodore Géricault
The Raft of the "Méduse," 1818–19
Musée du Louvre, Paris

and are the readier to meet it ourselves if we have studied Joseph Wright of Derby's *The Old Man and Death* (fig. 5). We have a deeper understanding of what it means for one person to give himself to another if we have studied Rembrandt's *The Jewish Bride* (fig. 6). We have a deeper understanding of what it means to love the world and lose it if we have studied the valedictory images of the dying Watteau. Marcel Proust was one of the most observant men who ever lived, but he spoke for all of us when he wrote, "Until I saw Chardin's paintings I never realized how much beauty lay around me in my parents' house, in the half-cleared table, in the corner of a tablecloth left awry, in the knife beside the empty oyster-shell."

Behind this collective confidence in art is our trust in the archetypal attitude, the stance before life, which is exemplified for us by each of the great masters in turn. It is a common dream that one man's life should be the measure of all things and that it should make sense of the complexity of experience in ways which are valid for everyone. Reading Tolstoy, watching a play by Shakespeare, working our way through the canon of Schubert's songs, looking at a Titian, or at a Dürer, or at Poussin's *Four Seasons,* we find that dream fulfilled. One man can master life. He cannot shield us from misfortune, but he can teach us to bear it better. And while we are under the spell of his art we feel invulnerable, as Brünnhilde was invulnerable when Wotan spread around her the magic circle of fire.

Invulnerability: that is what people ask of art. It would be a bad day if such achievements, and such men, could be talked about only in the past tense. No one likes to think that there lies before us only a long littleness. If rage and dismay enter so often into reactions to new art it is because of what is at stake: our capacity to make sense of life as it now presents itself. The Old Masters are still there, and they may well be present to us more vividly than many people whom we meet in "real life"; but we need the new masters, too, and it is very uncomfortable to feel that they may not be there.

The poet Charles Baudelaire realized this as early as the 1840s. He foresaw that the conditions of life were going to change faster and faster, and that the duty of modern art would be "to express that specific beauty which is intrinsic to our new emotions." Our *new* emotions, he said; for there were going to be new emotions to make new sense of. Baudelaire knew that there would be drastic readjustments for all, both in the public and in the private domain, and that art would have to come to terms with them. And that is what has happened; Tolstoy in his works said all that there is to say about many aspects of life, but we needed Solzhenitsyn to tell us in *Cancer Ward* and *The First Circle* how

5. Joseph Wright of Derby
The Old Man and Death, c. 1774
Wadsworth Atheneum, Hartford, Conn

6. Rembrandt van Ryn
The Jewish Bride (Isaac and Rebecca?)
Rijksmuseum, Amsterdam

7. Nicolas Poussin
Massacre of the Innocents (detail), 1630–31
Musée Condé, Chantilly

8. Edvard Munch
The Shriek, 1896 (lithograph,
after the painting of 1893)
The Museum of Modern Art,
New York

9. Pablo Picasso
The Charnel House, 1945
The Museum of Modern Art, New York

much of human dignity can survive when a great adventure is perverted and the vision of a just world brought to nothing. Beethoven in *Fidelio* gave us once and forever an ideal image of human loyalty; but not until Schoenberg's *Erwartung,* more than one hundred years later, did music yield a comparable image of the dissolution of personality under stress.

In art, equally, we had needs which could not be satisfied by the Old Masters, because those needs did not exist when the Old Masters were around. Poussin in his *Massacre of the Innocents* (fig. 7) gave us an unforgettable image of a human mouth wide open in a scream; but because he was a great classical artist that scream was incidental to his Olympian overview of the scene as a whole. It fell to Edvard Munch, in 1893 (fig. 8), to give us an image of a shriek which (in Munch's own words) "pierced the whole of Nature" and stood for a sudden, vast and quite irresistible sensation of panic and dismay. Europe needed just that picture at just that time, and nothing from the past could have taken its place. In 1945, when the complete facts about the Nazi concentration camps were available for the first time, Europe needed Picasso's *The Charnel House* (fig. 9), which was the more powerful for its sobriety of color, its condensed, pressed-down, claustrophobic imagery, and its refusal to itemize what was so readily to hand in print. The best art of the past hundred years came into being on occasions when nothing from the past would fill the bill. What those occasions were, and what art did about them, is the subject of this series.

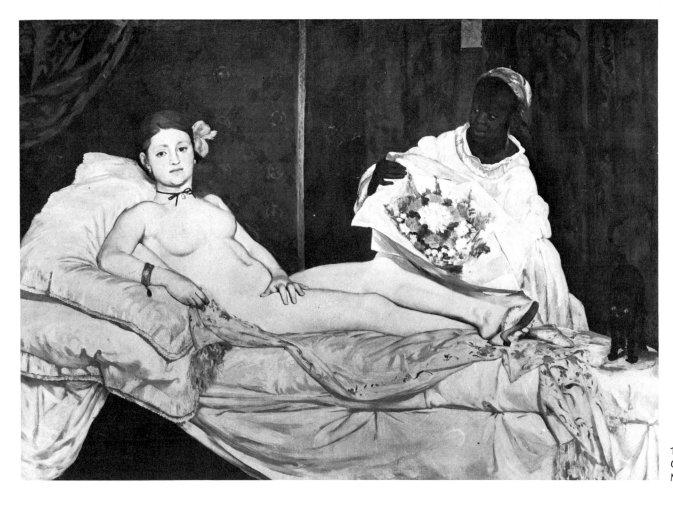

10. Edouard Manet
Olympia, 1863
Musée du Louvre, Paris

OLYMPIA—*A DECLARATION OF WAR*

As to exactly when new art came in and old art went out, several opinions can be upheld. There is a case for those who believe that the change came in the second half of the 1860s. Those five years were pregnant with the future: these were the years when Marx began to publish *Das Kapital,* Nobel invented dynamite and Bismarck drew nearer, step by step, to the domination of Europe. In painting, not-yet-named Impressionism was beginning to dissolve the Old Master tradition of modeling from dark to light in a simulated deep space. The "subject," as previously conceived, was giving way to a new conception of painting, in which the artist's sensations *were* the subject, no other being needed. One of the most challenging pictures of the century was put on view at the Paris Salon in 1865: *Olympia* by Edouard Manet (fig. 10). *Olympia* was challenging in every possible way. It stood

for a new kind of candor as between the painter and painting, as between the painter and his subject matter, and as between the painter and his public. Manet in 1863 had annoyed people very much by transposing motifs from the Old Masters into modern life and showing, in his *Le Déjeuner sur l'herbe* (fig. 13), how it was possible for a pretty young girl to take off all her clothes while picnicking in the open air with two fully dressed men. That painting had been rejected by the official Salon; but two years later *Olympia* was hung among the 3,559 canvases which had officialdom's sanction.

We do not, of course, see *Olympia* as our great-great-grandfathers would have seen it had they chanced to be in Paris in 1865. The picture has aged, as a physical object. Where once it looked blank and blatant it now looks what it is: an Old Master

7

11. Gustave Courbet
The Trellis, 1863
The Toledo Museum of Art, Toledo, Ohio

12. Pierre Auguste Renoir
Monet Painting in His Garden at Argenteuil, 1873
Wadsworth Atheneum, Hartford, Conn.

of our time. More than a hundred years of rougher, more coarsely provocative painting of the female nude has made us aware that Manet was essentially an aristocrat. We also know, as the public of the 1860s mostly did not, that the pose is taken from Titian's *Venus of Urbino,* which Manet had copied nine years earlier. The treatment of the naked figure now seems to us a model of tenderness and delicacy; but at the time it looked two-dimensional and incomplete ("Like the Queen of Spades just out of her bath," said Gustave Courbet). We enjoy the cat, and we find it wonderfully true to the facts of feline behavior, and we know the symbolic role of the cat in the poetry of Manet's friend Baudelaire. In fact, we find the whole picture strongly Baudelairean in its frankness, its overtones of luxury and indulgence, and in the contrast between the white of the flesh, the white of the sheets, the dazzling still life of the bouquet of flowers, and the dark face and hands of the attendant. We relish the uninhibited way in which the naked girl looks straight at us, as much as to say, "Here I am. What are you going to do about it?" The public of the 1860s sensed that the girl was saying it. But they also sensed, even if unconsciously, that the way of painting was saying it, too. *Olympia* was a declaration of war. The public was presented with a new way of seeing and a new way of setting down the thing seen. "Here I am," was the message, "and what are you going to do about it?" The mid-1860s were crucial in that respect. In 1867 both Manet and Courbet exhibited on their own at the World's Fair in Paris, thereby indicating that an alternative must soon be found to the art circuits of officialdom. These were the years in which Claude Monet and Pierre Auguste Renoir (fig. 12) began to paint regularly in the open air; and in which Camille Pissarro put it about that black and bitumen should be outlawed by every painter worthy of the name; and in which the young Zola began to champion the young Paul Cézanne. If we are simply looking for the new, we need look no further.

The case for the late 1860s is the stronger in that Impressionist paintings of the top class have made so great a contribution to human happiness. Looking at them, we think better of life and better of ourselves. Nor are they simply a school of pleasure, and one from which we have all graduated; they are also a school of truth. Impressionist painting was true to everyday experience in a way that painting had not been true before. This is how light falls, this is how color is broken up, this is how the fugitive moment presents itself. These pictures have a physical beauty, but they have a moral beauty as well: free and independent human beings have said "No" to pictorial tradition and set themselves instead to tell the truth about what happens when they set up their easels in front of Nature. It was the truth about what the eye

13. Edouard Manet
Le Déjeuner sur l'herbe, 1863
Musée du Louvre, Paris

Like many of Manet's paintings, the *Déjeuner sur l'herbe* was an imaginative mixture of observation from real life and reminiscences of Old Master painting. Initially prompted by the sight of women bathing in the Seine, and modeled by Manet's brother Eugène, his brother-in-law the Dutch sculptor Ferdinand Leenhoff, and his favorite subject, Victorine Meurend, the *Déjeuner* was based in part on an engraving after Raphael by Marcantonio Raimondi.

saw, and it was also the truth about what happened on the canvas. The all-over flicker of Impressionism mimed the very act of putting paint on canvas, where the suaver, blander and, in intention, seamless procedures of earlier painting had tended to conceal it. Impressionism said "No" to the mind, with its apparatus of received values, and put its trust in intuition. That does not sound, in today's terms, like too momentous an undertaking. But then we say things every day which would have got us banished or burned alive in earlier times; in art, equally, we take it for granted that we can do just as we like, with impunity. The painters of the 1860s were the prisoners of a very different set of historical conditions. Edmond Duranty, one of the most discerning of French writers on art, had said in 1855 that "It takes immense genius to represent, simply and sincerely, what we see in front of us." That had never been what art was about; for the tens of

14. Edouard Manet
Portrait of Emile Zola, 1868
Musée du Louvre, Paris

Emile Zola was one of the first people to speak out in favor of Manet's work, and Manet in 1868 returned the compliment by painting this portrait of Zola. It became famous not so much as a likeness of Zola himself, as for its brilliant passages of still life and its compact anthology of enthusiasms common to both men at the time: the Japanese silk screen, the Utamaro print, the photograph of Manet's *Olympia,* the engraving after Velázquez, the first edition of Zola's little book on Manet.

9

III. Edgar Degas
Café Singer Wearing a Glove, 1878
Fogg Art Museum, Cambridge, Mass.

11

15. Claude Monet
Bazille and Camille, c. 1865
National Gallery of Art, Washington, D.C.

were putting a completely new style of life at the disposal of everyone. At once rakish and imposing, convenient and yet the emblems of an imperious masculinity, they were the great new subject of the day. When Gustave Flaubert began to write *A Sentimental Education* in 1865, he chose for his opening scene the departure of a steamboat, with all its attendant bustle and activity, as a symbol for the way in which human relationships are continually forming and reforming. Manet in his *The Folkestone Boat, Boulogne,* 1869 (pl. I), and Monet in his painting of *The Gare Saint-Lazare, Paris,* 1877 (pl. II), found in the steam age an ideal subject matter. The scene on the quayside allowed Manet to employ what looked at the time like an almost improvisational method of composition; the rapid, nervous movement of the brush corresponded exactly to the vibration of the ship's engines, the brisk to-and-fro of passengers and crew, and the sense— never absent from the most conventional departure—that a decisive moment in life was at hand. People were about to pass from the known to the unknown, from *terra firma* to the open sea; and painting was in the same situation.

In Impressionist painting, the eye has a new privilege: that of concentrating on aspects of experience which had previously been thought to be too disorderly, too freakish, too seemingly accidental to qualify as material for art. Manet found this material on the quayside, where the spectacle changed from moment to moment. Monet, in the Gare Saint-Lazare series, took the huge iron-and-glass structure of the station, which had only lately been opened; he took the locomotives, which a generation earlier would have seemed like visions from an unimaginable future; and he took the element of steam itself—the mysterious, tinted exhalations which ballooned up and up beneath the unprecedented roof. The Gare Saint-Lazare was a startling enough sight even in the 1930s, when the steam locomotive had not yet been ousted; in the 1870s, and for painters who had known the countrified look of a pre-industrial Paris, there can have been nothing to cushion the shock of modernity.

But if Monet was painting the new world, he was also painting the new way. He was using the element of shock in the experience of the Gare Saint-Lazare to cover and justify the element of shock in Impressionism itself. In the picture reproduced here, for example, he used the swerving movement of the right-hand set of tracks in the foreground to draw the observer into the center of the painting. That center is defined as a space like a diamond laid on its side, with the flattened and inverted V of the roof as its top; the lower half of the diamond is formed by two invisible lines that run through the upper section of the two locomotives in the foreground and meet up in the spectral locomotive that

thousands of people who went every year to the official Salons in Paris, art was one of the learned professions, and it was not the function of the artist to teach people to look around them.

The Impressionists thought just the contrary. They were living in an extraordinary time: a time when the conditions of life were changing more radically than in any previous era. They saw, for instance, that between them the steam train and the steamboat

12

can be glimpsed in the center and at the rear. Within this diamond is the true subject of the painting: the play of light on something never before recorded—the iridescent cloudscape of steam as it forms and reforms within a confined space. Such a thing had never been seen before, and it will now never be seen again.

No one relished the new subject matter of Impressionism more completely than Edgar Degas, in the series of music-hall and café-concert studies which he made in the second half of the 1870s. In the café-concert he found an ideal combination of the things that most prompted his imagination—faces and bodies in vigorous movement, artificial lighting that turned the most humdrum scene into carnival, strange and aggressive combinations of color. The scene lent itself to abrupt, asymmetrical, snapshot-like images which threw the emphasis everywhere but where it was expected. It was a continual challenge; faced with hard-working professionals, Degas in his turn gave all that he had.

A capital example of this is the *Café Singer Wearing a Glove* of 1878 (pl. III). Degas at this time was using tempera mixed with pastel to produce little paintings, at once astringent and feather-soft, which he could carry through quickly after long and careful preparation. "Pastel colors" in everyday speech have connotations of the washed-out and the effete; but there was nothing of that when Degas matched palest lilac against salmon pink, as here, and set up a sharp apple green to sing out against the black of the glove. Where other painters might have portrayed the singer as a dignified figure in the middle distance, Degas gives us a dentist's view of her wide-open mouth, allows her to slip sideways as if at any moment she would move out of the frame altogether, turns her black glove into the most powerful single image in the picture, and makes of her outstretched and bent-back thumb an unforgettable image of effort and strain. Degas spared nobody; but he didn't diminish anybody, either.

Man, as a seeing animal, has few monuments that can compare with the masterpieces of Impressionism. But man is not only a seeing animal. He is also a thinking, an imagining, a cross-referring and a systems-making animal; and none of these latter traits could be accommodated by pure Impressionism.

Impressionism was by definition dependent on the fugitive and the contingent in human experience. The beauty of the sunlight on the climbing path in the painting of that name by Pissarro (pl. V) is something that once seen is never forgotten; we see such things, ever after, as he saw them. But there are other kinds of experience, and other ways of marshaling them; and to the extent that Impressionism cannot deal with them it has, in the end, its limitations.

16. Claude Monet
The River, 1868
The Art Institute of Chicago

When Cézanne said of Monet that he was "only an eye—but what an eye!" he did not mean to put Monet down. An uncorrupted eye is a wonderful thing, and many a later painter has set a very high value on Monet's robust energy, on his open and candid procedures, and on his readiness to break with the past when instinct told him that it was the right thing to do. Where Manet hedged his bets on modernity with learned allusions to this great master or that, Monet simply went ahead on his own. He was a master of the single idea. But to the extent that a great compound idea is more resonant in the end than a great single idea, I myself would nominate the late 1880s as the moment at which new art came in and old art went out.

What I mean is this: nothing could be more delectable than the masterpieces of Impressionism. But a work of art is not simply an object of delectation; it is also an ideas-bank. A work of art is an emblem of the good life, but it is also an energy system. The ideas and the energy in question are not those of the artist alone, though he may well be uniquely alert to them; there is no warrant for the legend of the major artist as a man who acts on inspirations peculiar to himself and owes nothing to earlier art.

IV. Pierre Auguste Renoir
The Luncheon of the Boating Party, 1881
The Phillips Collection, Washington, D.C.

Renoir's *The Luncheon of the Boating Party* is by any count one of the masterpieces of Impressionism. In its size, in its complexity, in the evident grandeur of its ambition, it measures itself against the great figure paintings of the European past. It has a glorious physicality: this is how life ought to be, but so seldom is. In the last resort there is, however, something plotted and contrived about it. In his attempt to rival the Old Masters,

Renoir had to jettison the instantaneity of pure Impressionism; the picture is not seen in one moment of time, as had happened with earlier, smaller, Impressionist paintings. It must, rather, have been built up in Old Master style and edited in the studio. Renoir put into it all that he had; two years later he decided that he had "gone to the end of Impressionism."

14

THE FATEFUL DECADE

So the place, the time and the current ideas all had their part to play in the 1880s. When the period is one of crisis and the current ideas are outstandingly rich and complex, the role of the place becomes decisive. It is a very great help to make art in a place which has had an uninterrupted tradition of great art for several hundred years *and is still producing it*. There was not much to be said for being a painter in Madrid after the death of Goya, or in Venice after the death of Tiepolo, since in both cities a great tradition then collapsed. But in Paris the tradition held firm and was never firmer than in the second half of the 19th century.

In the 1880s, a world new beyond all prediction was coming up over the horizon. Not for many years did people learn to make the right cross-references among all that was going on. Certainly there was a large audience for the three-word pronouncement "God is dead" when it came out as part of Nietzsche's *Gay Science* (1882–87). But few people can have foreseen that Krafft-Ebing's *Psychopathia Sexualis* (1886) would cast so long a shadow into the 20th century, or that that century would look back with awe to the paper with which in 1881, as a young man of only 25, J. J. Thomson set physics on a new path. The Michelson–Morley experiment of 1887 established, among other things, that there is no such thing as the absolute velocity of a material body, as distinct from the relative velocity of any two material bodies. As such, it was not without its parallels in the work of Cézanne, where the identity of any given object is often most subtly varied and adjusted by the fact of its proximity to other given objects. The historian of ideas should point also to Freud's meetings in Paris in the winter of 1885–86 with Charcot, the great specialist for cases of hysteria, which led eventually to a completely new phase in our understanding of human nature. Few knew of all this, just as even at the turn of the century there were reputable histories of French literature which did not mention Rimbaud's *Illuminations,* first published in 1887.

Ibsen and Strindberg in the 1880s were dynamiting pretty well every accepted idea of private and public morality, even if plays like *Ghosts* (1881), *An Enemy of the People* (1882), *Rosmersholm* (1886), *The Father* (1887) and *Miss Julie* (1888) were not widely seen till the 1890s and Strindberg was known to his friends in Paris less as a dramatist than as a keen and perceptive student of painting. The emergence in 1888 of the word "chromosome" signaled an important shift, elsewhere, in human understanding. Given as a name to the minute bodies which had been detected in the dividing cells of which animals and plants are composed, it led directly to one of the most significant generalizations

17. Edvard Munch
August Strindberg, 1896
The Museum of Modern Art, New York

18. Edvard Munch
Henrik Ibsen in the Grand Café, Christiania, 1902
Munch-museet, Oslo

In Paris in 1896 Munch for a time lived next door to the dramatist August Strindberg. Two such hypersensitive natures were bound to conflict: "I am sure you want to kill me," Strindberg once wrote to Munch, "but I shall prevent it. You are not to become my murderer."

Munch's relations with Henrik Ibsen were notably more harmonious. When Munch's work was received with derision in 1895, Ibsen said to him, "You will find, as I have found, that the more enemies one has, the more friends one has, also."

19. Adolf von Menzel
*The Departure of Kaiser Wilhelm from Berlin on July 31, 1870, to Join the
   Troops at the Front*
Nationalgalerie, Berlin

in modern biology—the chromosome–gene theory, which posits
that all living things have a common unit of structure. Once
again, science and art turned out to have affinities as yet unsus-
pected. Such things were crucial in their field—as was, for that
matter, the publication in 1890 of the first two volumes of J. G.
Frazer's *The Golden Bough*. Imminent and radical changes could
be descried in almost every department of life, and more especially in our notions of human nature, of space, time and cau-
sality, and of the structure of the universe and the structure of
ourselves.

There were, furthermore, elements in the general situation
which every intelligent person should have been able to de-
cipher. From the time of the Franco-Prussian war in 1870–71 it
had been clear that Europe was bent on tearing itself apart. The
French financial crisis of 1882 was trifling by the standards of the
crash of 1929, but it was unpleasant enough for those—Gauguin
among them—who earned their living by the stock market. Kro-
potkin's *Paroles d'un Révolté* (1884) was one of many signs of
radical activity in Europe. In Russia the increased persecution of
the Jews, in Germany Bismarck's demands for an ever larger
army, in Africa the establishment of the Congo state as the per-

sonal property of King Leopold II of the Belgians—all these were
events of the 1880s that went on reverberating well into our own
century. The world was getting into big trouble, quite clearly. All
over Europe broad new boulevards were being cut through capital cities; but to what purpose? And what kind of life would be
led in those cities? No one knew, but everyone was free to guess.
People looked at the mechanized armies, and they heard about
the ironclad warships, and they saw the armed police going out
about their business, and they knew something—not too much,
but something—about the plight of the disinherited masses. They
could draw their own conclusions.

Art would not be art—would not, that is to say, be one of the
most acutely indicative barometers of human activities—if it did
not react, and did not adjust, to a situation of that sort. Very great
and quite new ambitions were forced upon art in the 1880s, and
the question to be answered was: what language would be ade-
quate for these ambitions? Did it exist already, or must it be
created?

It was a good question. Impressionism had proved that great
art could be made from the most ordinary experiences, with no
references to earlier art, no deft allusions to the Bible or Virgil
or Ariosto, no search for "significance" in subject matter. Even
so, its prime characteristic was a certain passivity before the
free-flowing, unstructured *données* of optical experience: the
donnée, the thing given, was the only thing that it took account
of. This had its heroic side: the glorious impartiality of Pissarro's
procedures had not been achieved overnight. Zola got the point
of Pissarro when he wrote of his *Jallais Hill, Pontoise* in 1867 (fig.
20) that "a beautiful picture by this artist is the work of an honest
man. I cannot better define his talent."

"Perhaps we all come out of Pissarro" was how Cézanne
summed up the matter. But it was not enough to come out; they
had to have somewhere to go afterward, and they also had to
have a greater freedom of maneuver than Impressionism could
offer. The future of mankind and the future of art both called for
that freedom. Only someone who was close to art and to artists
could intuit the extent to which art was about to lose, one by
one, the near-monopolies which it had enjoyed for centuries.
The swing away from Impressionism was above all an instinctive,
unstudied defense against art's then-imminent losses; a survival
strategy for art, and a removal to positions in which art could
keep its place as one of the most meaningful of human activities.

To count up the losses in question, we have only to look at the
position today and see how many of art's former prerogatives
have vanished. In the lifetime of Titian or Rembrandt it was a rare
and an almost magical experience for people to come into con-

20. Camille Pissarro
Jallais Hill, Pontoise, 1867
The Metropolitan Museum of
Art, New York

tact with images at all, outside of a church. Till well into the 19th century the European street was for the most part a matter of bare walls and long empty prospects with only a house number or the name of a tradesman to animate the scene. Any metropolitan photograph of 1885 or later (figs. 21 and 22) will show the difference. Our lives today are spent in almost continual contact with images of one sort or another. In all this, art's privileges have been withdrawn, one by one. For fact, people go to the newspaper, the newsmagazine, or the television screen. For fancy, they go to the movies. Since Freud, the unified, unhesitating procedures of formal portraiture look obsequious and incomplete; the camera's offhand stalking seems to us almost always to give more truthful results. After the great war-photographers (fig. 25) battle-paintings look stagey and squeamish. Even Eternity has been taken from art; and as for our place in the universe, a cam-

era set down on the moon is more compelling than anything that art can come up with. In these contexts art has for years been a second-class activity.

If those contexts had been the only ones in which art could operate, painting and sculpture would long ago have abdicated, moved to the peripheries of life, accepted the archaic status of handweaving or bespoke shoemaking or gone down altogether, the way the Alexandrine vanished from the theater when people wanted a more informal way of speaking from the stage. We owe it to Courbet, Manet, Monet, Pissarro and Degas that this was never really in question, and to Cézanne, Georges Seurat, Vincent van Gogh and Paul Gauguin that in the late 1880s a whole set of new options was opened for art.

Not many people cared at the time. For one reason or another the work was not easy to see, and Authority was in no hurry to

17

V. Camille Pissarro
The Climbing Path at the Hermitage, Pontoise, 1875
The Brooklyn Museum

18

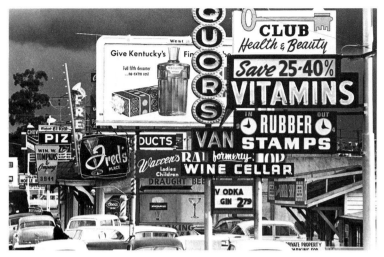

21. (*left*) Edward Anthony
Broadway on a Rainy Day, 1859 (stereograph)
George Eastman House, Rochester, N.Y.

22. (*above*) Rondal Partridge
El Camino Real, Palo Alto, California (photograph)

Landscapes like the one on the opposite page now look to us like Arcadia. Even Broadway, in 1859, had still a pre-industrial look. But by the 1960s—see this California townscape—the no longer innocent eye was being bombarded night and day by insistent images.

relieve the condition of physical and moral isolation in which Cézanne, van Gogh and Gauguin were working. Authority was at best indifferent, at worst actively dismissive: Nietzsche could have had Cézanne in mind when he wrote in 1885, "It is not the strength, but the duration, of great sentiments that makes great men."

Officialdom was quite right, from its own point of view. Napoleon III judged his interests correctly when he took his whip to a painting by Courbet. Kaiser Wilhelm II knew best when he fired the director of his National Gallery for buying too many modern pictures. Kaiser Francis Joseph had second sight when he told his coachman never to drive past a new and wholly unornamented building by Adolf Loos. These sovereigns knew what Plato knew: that the state of art is bound up with the state of society, and that when the laws of art change the laws of the state are likely to change with them. Courbet was a republican, a free-thinker, a friend of Proudhon, the anarcho-socialist philosopher who in-

vented the phrase "property is theft." He detested everything that emperors stand for, and he was later to go to jail for his beliefs. The Emperors and the Kaisers were absolutely right when they sensed that there was an imminent shift in the laws of art, and that imminent shift stood for a freer, more spontaneous, more independent and less biddable state of mind—just the sort of thing that emperors should be nervous of. Authority thrives on submission, and the message of art in the late 1880s was that each man should decide for himself how to live.

What Then Must We Do? The title of Tolstoy's little book, written in 1886, could stand as motto for the whole decade. Both van Gogh and Gauguin were obsessed with the implications of that title—so much so, in fact, that when Gauguin came to sum up his whole career in the huge painting which is now in the Boston Museum of Fine Arts, he gave it a name which has a slashing, panoramic, Tolstoyan quality: *Whence do we come? What are we? Where are we going?* (fig. 33).

19

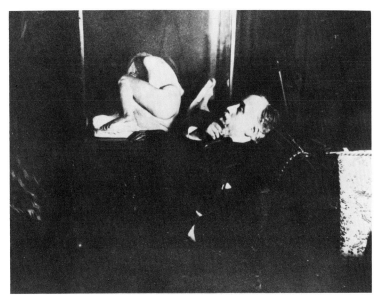

23. Edgar Degas
Degas seated, with sculpture in the background (photograph)
The Metropolitan Museum of Art, New York

24. Abel Gance
Antonin Artaud as Marat, in a scene from *Napoléon,* 1926 (film still)
The Museum of Modern Art, New York
    Film Stills Archive

26. Irving Penn
Colette, Paris, 1951
(photograph)
The Museum of
Modern Art,
New York

25. Robert Capa
"Collaborationist," Chartres, France, 1944 (photograph)
The Museum of Modern Art, New York

Art and photography have been feeding upon one another ever since the days when Degas, that master of the casual-seeming pose, experimented with photographs of himself. In 1926, when Abel Gance made his epic movie *Napoléon,* and Antonin Artaud was cast as Marat, Gance borrowed directly from J. L. David's painting (fig. 2) for the climactic scene of the murder of Marat by Charlotte Corday. In our own time, no painter can rival the immediacy with which a great news photographer documents the happenings of the day: in *"Collaborationist," Chartres, 1944,* Robert Capa fixed forever the moment at which women who had fraternized with German soldiers were having their heads shaved, all over France. In portraiture, likewise, the painter is now very rare who could challenge the humane insight of Irving Penn's portrait of the then 78-year-old Colette, author of some of the most memorable of modern French novels and stories.

27. Edward Penfield
Harper's March, 1897
The Museum of Modern Art, New York

28. (*right*) Pierre Bonnard
Screen, 1897 (lithograph in four panels)
The Museum of Modern Art, New York

In his lithographed poster for *Harper's* magazine, the American poster maker Edward Penfield came remarkably close to the motif of stationary horse-drawn cabs, which Pierre Bonnard used over and over again in the 1890s and apotheosized in the four-part screen which he painted in 1892–94 and remade as a color lithograph in 1897. In each case the motif of the cabs was "hung" at the top of the sheet in an elegant, offhand way which probably derived in the first place from the study of Japanese prints.

29. (*below*) Thomas Eakins
Miss Amelia van Buren, c. 1891 (photograph)
Philadelphia Museum of Art

30. Thomas Eakins
*Portrait of Miss Amelia
van Buren*, 1889–91
The Phillips Collection,
Washington, D.C.

Thomas Eakins is, by common consent, the greatest American painter of the 19th century. He was also, from 1880 onward, an enthusiastic photographer; and there was often a significant interplay between his paintings and his photographs—as here, left and above, for instance, in the two likenesses of his pupil and friend, Amelia van Buren.

31. Paul Gauguin
Self-Portrait with Halo, 1889
National Gallery of Art, Washington, D.C.

Gauguin's histrionic side comes out strongly in this painting, which shows him as Lucifer, leader of the fallen angels, with the symbols of his position all around him: the serpent of temptation, the apples of knowledge, the ironical halo.

32. Vincent van Gogh
Self-Portrait, 1888
Fogg Art Museum, Cambridge, Mass.

Tolstoy's *What I Believe In* came out in French in 1882, and one of the people to whom its ideas appealed especially was van Gogh. "Tolstoy suggests," he wrote to his brother Theo, "that whatever may happen in the way of a violent revolution there will also be a private and secret revolution in man. From this there will be born a new religion—or rather something entirely new, for which we do not have a name. It will give comfort, and make life possible, in the way that Christianity once did."

This idea mattered a great deal to van Gogh, who had tried his very best to be an evangelist and had had no success at all. Better than many a more worldly individual, he understood the apoca-

33. Paul Gauguin
Whence do we come? What are we? Where are we going? 1897
Museum of Fine Arts, Boston

Gauguin began work on this huge canvas at a time when he could be in no doubt that, as he wrote to a friend in November, 1897, his days were numbered. "Living and partly living" on mangoes, guavas and an occasional shrimp, with no money to buy bread and a steadily worsening physical condition, he nonetheless put such strength as he had into a three-part panorama which would sum up certain themes which had long preoccupied him. "The landscape," he wrote later, "is blue and Veronese green from one end to the other, and the naked figures stand out against it in bold orange." The general theme of the painting is the irresponsibility, the ignorance of destiny, the

general lack of focus and understanding, which leads human beings to go on living in an aimless day-to-day way while inscrutable forces, far stronger than ourselves, look down on us.

It was, Gauguin said, "a philosophical work, comparable to the Gospels." He admitted that it had "enormous mathematical faults"; but he refused to adjust them, prizing above any mere correctness the fact that the big picture had been done "direct from imagination, straight from the brush, on sackcloth full of knots and wrinkles." In a letter written some years after the picture was completed, Gauguin summarized the subject matter by saying that in the left-hand section an old woman sits, near to death; that in the central section "the man of instinct," still in his prime, meditates on the meaning of human existence; and that in the right-hand section life begins again with a little child lying beside a stream.

lyptic implications of industrialization. He was convinced that "through revolutions, through war, through the bankruptcy of worm-eaten states, disasters are bound to fall like a terrible lightning on the modern world and on civilization." But what if art could bring about the "private and secret revolution" which Tolstoy had in mind? What if he, van Gogh, could help to avert disaster by touching men's hearts with his paintings as he had once hoped to touch them with his words? Van Gogh died before he could see his pictures put on show; but when we look at the lines of people which stretch round the block when those pictures are on exhibition today, we know that he did indeed get through to them.

SEURAT—AN ARTIST'S ARTIST

More could be got out of art: as to that, the dreamer and the scientist were of one mind with the student of society. Art's potential had been underrated, underused, undersystematized. Art was not a buttonhole to be worn once a year; it was, on the contrary, one of the most fundamental of human activities. So that Seurat was aiming high, but not too high, when he said that he wanted his studies of metropolitan life to be the modern equivalent of the Panathenaeic frieze on the Parthenon. The Parisians, like all other peoples, revealed themselves in their pleasures; and it was in their pleasures that Seurat sought them

34. Camille Pissarro
The River Oise near Pontoise, 1873
Sterling and Francine Clark Art Institute, Williamstown, Mass.

Pissarro in this painting pioneered the idea that the industrial scene was not necessarily an affront to the dignity of art but could, in the right hands, be made to look as beautiful as any other. Seurat was the later, greater champion of this notion; but Pissarro in this instance was ten years ahead of him.

out—*en masse* on a hot summer Sunday afternoon, in *La Grande Jatte* (fig. 37), in ones and twos in *Une Baignade à Asnières* (1883–84), at the theater in *Le Chahut* (fig. 35), at the circus in the painting of that name, and at the street fair in *La Parade* (pl. VI).

Seurat was only 31 when he died. His output of oil paintings was small by comparison with that of van Gogh or Gauguin, and he has none of their universal celebrity. There are those who find his speckly procedures mechanical; even in his lifetime he is reputed to have been called "the little chemist" on account of the deliberate, laboratorylike manner in which he calculated the dosage of this color or that. Nor did the dot prove to be in itself a very rewarding instrument in the hands of others.

There is, even so, a grotesque injustice in this view of Seurat. Of course he was an eager theoretician. Like many another clever man in the 1880s, he believed that applied science could do a great deal for art. To that end, he studied the composition of color, and the emotional properties of mathematics, and the sig-

35. Georges Seurat
Le Chahut, 1890
Rijksmuseum Kröller-
Müller, Otterlo, Holland

36. Jules Chéret
*Les Girard, L'Horloge,
Champs-Elysées,* 1879
The Museum of Modern
Art, New York

Jules Chéret designed over 1,200 posters from 1869 onward. He excelled above all with effects of dynamic energy and in *Les Girard* he drew on memories of American circus posters which he had seen on a visit to England. Ten years later a great painter, Georges Seurat, carried the high-kicking image a stage further in a painting called *Le Chahut* (fig. 35).

37. Georges Seurat
Sunday Afternoon on the Island of La Grande Jatte, 1884–86
The Art Institute of Chicago

nificance of ascending and descending lines, and many another para- or pseudo-scientific formulation. Above all, he believed, as the French theoretician David Sutter had argued in his *Phenomena of Vision* in 1880, that "the laws of color harmony can be learned as one learns the laws of harmony in music." In this Seurat followed a number of earlier French 19th-century theoreticians, but with the difference that where their vision of a grammar of the arts did not really get off the printed page, Seurat

was one of the great picture-architects of all time. He was also a penetrating social observer, with a particularly keen eye for the compulsive pranks to which his contemporaries subjected themselves in the name of pleasure. The governing principle behind his metropolitan subjects was this: that places do things to people, and that new kinds of places do new kinds of things to them, and that it is the painter's privilege to sort all this out.

La Parade is full of scientific devices. The idea of using the dot as a basic unit was in line with the 19th century's many attempts to estimate the size of the smallest unit of matter into which physical phenomena can be broken down. Baudelaire in 1846 was already analyzing Nature in terms of its molecular structure and likening it, in its color relations, to "a spinning-top which revolves so rapidly that it looks gray, even though it embraces within itself the entire gamut of color"; and Seurat's contemporaries noted that although he applied his colors in small touches of the utmost purity and intensity, the optical mix which resulted often had the grayish look which Baudelaire attributed to Nature in its molecular aspect.

In its architectural construction, *La Parade* is based on mathematical theories put forward in 1885 by a Frenchman called Charles Henry, who was regarded at that time as a universal genius, as ready to pronounce on the best method of training for a bicycle race as on whatever lofty and abstract question was the topic of the day. A pleasure–pain theory much in favor in the 1880s can be linked to Seurat's use of a meandering line here and there, just as the form of the gas lamps at the top of the painting corresponds to the idiosyncratic, flowerlike forms that Seurat prized as an emblem of festivity.

Art history thrives on details such as this. But the real message of the painting relates more to the dehumanization of big-city life than to systematic ingenuities of color and line. Anyone who compares an earlier treatment of the same theme—Gabriel de Saint-Aubin's *La Parade du boulevard* (fig. 38), for instance—will see that where Saint-Aubin speaks for genuine, unforced, unsophisticated enjoyment, Seurat is almost ghoulish in his detailing of the metropolitan scene. His trombone player might be an executioner, and his auxiliary musicians defendants on the stand, while the director of the circus, in his cutaway coat, might be a prison warden ready to strike out at the nearest offender with his cane. Artificial light pollutes the environment, and the scene as a whole reminds us of what had lately been published in Rimbaud's *Illuminations*—the portrait of a big modern city as a place where trees bear no leaf, where people prefer not to know one another, and where the air is fouled by the leavings of industry. (On this last subject, Seurat's drawings of Paris have much to say.) *La Parade* is a masterpiece of ordered statement; but it also calls for a change of heart before the big city gets out of hand.

Seurat looked in many directions: back to Piero della Francesca, out of the studio window to the posters by Chéret (fig. 36) which were turning the boulevards into one enormous picture gallery, and forward toward kinds of art as yet unimagined. The ramifying tendrils of Art Nouveau derived in part from Seurat's use of arabesque; Marcel Duchamp, in his *Nude Descending a*

38. Gabriel-Jacques de Saint-Aubin
A Street Show in Paris (La Parade du boulevard)
The National Gallery, London

Staircase, developed an idea of serial representation which was already present in Seurat's *Le Chahut*; Paul Klee by 1912 had mastered Seurat's color doctrine, even though his own work was then still primarily in black and white; Robert Delaunay took the systemic use of pure divided color and worked it up into Orphism; Wassily Kandinsky wrote that Seurat had aimed to show "not a fragment of Nature chosen at random, but Nature complete and entire in all her splendor"; and although Henri Matisse did not go along with the programmatic element in Seurat's work, he saluted "those other, truer values—those human painterly values which today seem ever more profound."

VI. Georges Seurat
Invitation to the Side-Show (La Parade), 1887–88
The Metropolitan Museum of Art, New York

39. Georges Seurat
Place de la Concorde, Winter, 1882–83
The Solomon R. Guggenheim Museum, New York

40. Paul Cézanne
Portrait of Camille Pissarro,
c. 1873
Mr. and Mrs. John Rewald,
New York

41. Camille Pissarro
Portrait of Cézanne, 1874
S. P. Avery Collection, The New
York Public Library

CÉZANNE—THE EXPERIENCE OF SEEING

It would be hard to work up much opposition today to the proposition that Cézanne was one of the greatest painters, and by extension of that one of the greatest men, who ever lived. No one has had more influence on later art. Yet a mature painting by Cézanne has neither the immaculate and inexorable organization of a painting by Seurat nor the importunate pull of a painting by van Gogh or Gauguin. The subject matter is likely to be sober and conventional; the manner was for a long time thought to be tentative and overlaid with second thoughts. (Cézanne "couldn't draw," people said.)

This was because Cézanne had dismantled, one by one, the beliefs on which the practice of art had previously been based. That was in itself so momentous an ambition that he did not need, and could not have encompassed, the hectic high color and the patently symbolical subject matter of Gauguin or van Gogh.

There was nothing in Cézanne of the willful iconoclast. He revered the French classic tradition—as it had been exemplified by Poussin, above all. He revered it for its clarity, its complex, masterful organization, its noble and fastidious utterance, its disdain for the private and the accidental. Everything in Poussin happens the way it is meant to happen; never does he permit himself a loose end, a second thought, a momentary whim or caprice. A price was paid for all this, as it was paid in the plays of Poussin's near-contemporary, Racine. In Racine, nobody sneezes; the disorder of everyday life is outlawed by classic tradition. In Poussin, equally, we never come across a passage that is awkward or unfinished or a piece of drawing that has evidently been flubbed.

Cézanne was alive to all this, but he knew that it was his destiny both to let in the things that had been left out of the French classic tradition and to let drop, one by one, its grave certainties. "Is that really how we look at the world? Or is there something in the nature of painting itself which has not yet been explored?" Those were the questions which Cézanne was to ask, and to answer, in the paintings of his last 29 years. He did not ask them in an abstract or schematic way. He *lived them*, in front of the motifs which Nature provided. No painter was ever more attentive to the outward and ostensible subject of his paintings: the portraits, the still lifes, the Provençal landscapes whose beauty Cézanne hoped to reveal for the first time. But fundamentally from the late 1870s onward he was also preoccupied with the notion of painting as a constructive act.

Cézanne took nothing for granted. He knew that style in art is like style in life: there is a moment at which it allows us to do

42. Paul Cézanne
Still Life with Apples, 1895–98
The Museum of Modern Art,
New York

what we have never done before, and there is a later moment at which it simply walls up the unknown and cuts us off from our own potentialities. Cézanne took down that wall; and he worked not as a dynamiter works but minutely and patiently, chip by chip, until in the end everything could come in. Prizing above all things a certain equilibrium of the vital faculties, Cézanne never aimed to let instinct rip. It must, for instance, have been very painful for him when he gradually came to realize that traditional perspective would have to go. He knew how for more than four hundred years perspective had been the painter's automatic pilot, marshaling on his behalf no matter how large a quantity of visual information. By taking as its first premise a single point of vision, perspective had stabilized visual experience. It had bestowed order on chaos; it allowed elaborate and systematized cross-referencing, and quite soon it had become a touchstone of coherence and even-mindedness. To "lose all sense of perspective" is to this day a synonym for mental collapse. Yet perspective, before Cézanne, was fundamentally one of the sanctified frauds that keeps the world turning: a conspiracy to deceive, in other words.

Of course it had brought great rewards. The expressive potential of perspective had been enormous. Cézanne acknowledged that his ambition was "to do Poussin over again from Nature"; and nothing in Western art is more moving than the godlike assurance with which Poussin (fig. 44) argues that perspective is the right and natural way, the harmonious and logical way, in which complex statements can be spelled out on canvas. Yet Cézanne had in mind something more truly and more completely expressive of human capacities. He was not an intellectual and it is very unlikely that he knew to what extent his stance before life was

29

43. (*above*) Paul Cézanne
Mont Ste. Victoire Seen from Bibemus Quarry,
  c. 1898–1900
The Baltimore Museum of Art

44. (*right*) Nicolas Poussin
Landscape with St. John at Patmos, 1645–50
The Art Institute of Chicago

characteristic of his time—and, more especially, of the attitude defined by Henri Bergson in a famous essay of 1889 on the nature of intuition: *Les Données immédiates de la conscience.* "We have to express ourselves in words," Bergson begins, "but most often we think in space." In French the word *conscience* means "conscience" in our sense, and it also means both "consciousness" and "knowledge." To a Frenchman, therefore, consciousness *is* knowledge, and to be conscious is to be learning, continuously. Bergson's ideas about duration and contingency, and about the interrelations and interpenetrations of objects, are often strikingly similar to Cézanne's procedures. We soon realize that whereas Tolstoy in the 1880s was asking "What Then Must We Do?" Cézanne was asking, "What can we know?" and asking it in terms which will always be relevant.

He let in, one by one, the things that had been kept out of painting: the fact, for instance, that in our knowledge of a given object time plays a part. We do not see it once and for all from a given point; nor does the given object have a given identity, once and for all. Monet also was aware of this, in his Cathedrals series of 1894; but the particularity of Cézanne was that he could

work the effects of serial vision into a single canvas, thereby showing how everything is relative, in questions of identity, and subject to time, and movement, and change. Renaissance and post-Renaissance practice had given art stability; but stability and equilibrium are not necessarily the same, and when stability is spurious—willed, that is to say, and arbitrary—bluff enters into it. Cézanne called that bluff.

It was the same bluff that lay behind all the other pseudo-immutable systems—Euclidean geometry, for one, and Newtonian physics, for another. All the bluffs got called, between 1880 and 1914, and nowhere more thoroughly than in art.

Cézanne rebuilt the experience of seeing. He rebuilt it on the canvas, touch by touch, and he made each touch do a three-fold duty. It had to be true to the object seen. It had to be true to the experience of seeing it. And it had to play its part in a grand overall design. That design was not carried out in the sweeping, unified and clearly eloquent style of the earlier masters. It was *built up,* piecemeal. All this is shown to perfection in his *Still Life with Peppermint Bottle* (pl. VII), which is a majestic amalgam of traits derived from French classical tradition, on the one hand,

30

VII. Paul Cézanne
Still Life with Peppermint Bottle
National Gallery of Art, Washington, D.C.

45. Paul Cézanne
The Card Players, 1890–92
The Metropolitan Museum
of Art, New York

and forays into completely new territory, on the other. Since the 17th century French still-life painting had been remarkable for the weight, the solidity, and the sense of a classical equilibrium, with which household objects were rendered. Cézanne was faithful to this: never was fruit more monumental, never glass more artfully transparent, never the neck and shoulder of a bottle more thoughtfully aligned to their surroundings.

But there was no authority in classical French painting for the peremptory way in which the top of the table had become invisible and illegible; for the way in which the decanter was made to belly out on the right; for the tumult of the drapes, which rear up from the top of the table like waves on a rough day at sea; or for the way in which the composition as a whole is both a por-

trait of stability, in which everything is balanced, somewhere and somehow, by every other thing, and at the same time a portrait of perpetual motion. Those drapes did not come from earlier painting but from the recesses of a riotous imagination; and yet, as always, Cézanne was minutely attentive to such details as the particular shiny red of the seal at the top of the bottle. There are portents of later painting in the way, for instance, in which the drapes mysteriously form, in the lower right-hand folds, into the likeness of a musical instrument much favored by the Cubists. There is a quick-moving, widely ranging system of echoes in the patterning of the drapes; Matisse was to pick this up and use it to great effect before 1914. Paintings such as this one stand on a high plateau between the past and the future of European paint-

46. Paul Cézanne
Le Château Noir, 1904–06
The Museum of Modern Art, New York

47. Louis Le Nain
Peasants in a Landscape, c. 1641
Wadsworth Atheneum, Hartford, Conn.

ing. Cézanne was always true to what Bergson called *la conscience immédiate:* the facts of his own awareness. Anyone who doubts this should look at his monumental and yet totally human *The Card Players* (fig. 45); each one of them is, as D. H. Lawrence said of one of his characters, "like a piece of the out-of-doors come indoors." Cézanne never took a formula from stock; every mark on the canvas had to prove itself. But he also personified the organizing intelligence; and as he grew older there developed an ever greater tension between the demands of this organizing intelligence and the evidence which was brought to an eye that grew continually more acute. It was a part of the French tradition that order and stillness and lucidity should be bestowed on scenes which in themselves were in continual flux. When Louis Le Nain painted his *Peasants in a Landscape* (fig. 47), for instance, he devised a grand mathematical structure for his figures; his picture is a triumph of the grand style, and yet it does not abate the individuality of his subjects. Their dignity as human beings is enhanced by it. When Corot painted his *Breton Women at a Well* (fig. 48), he too gave the scene a severe, pyramidal structure in which the element of chance was ruled out. Cézanne, in the big *Grandes Baigneuses* now in Philadelphia (pl. VIII), was as concerned as either of his predecessors with the august harmo-

48. Jean Baptiste Camille Corot
Breton Women at a Well, 1850–55
Musée du Louvre, Paris

VIII. Paul Cézanne
Grandes Baigneuses, 1898–1905
Philadelphia Museum of Art

34

nies of triangular form—in fact he used the triangle three times over: once in the trees and twice among the bathers—but he also let in all the paradoxes, the contradictions and the irrational emphases which abound in our everyday experience. Cézanne included these too, and in doing so he gave altogether grander dimensions both to art itself and to the cognitive act. It is for this reason that Cézanne now seems to have given us, in words used by Henry James in another context, "the strongest dose of life that art can give, and the strongest dose of art that life can give."

That quotation might seem to relate, and in its original context in *The Tragic Muse* did relate, to a key moment in classical drama, when violent emotion is made bearable, but only just, by art. In Cézanne it might seem to apply more to the early imaginative subjects, where rape and murder are taken for granted, than to the work of the later years. But Cézanne from the 1880s onward was on to one of the fundamental truths about our life on earth: that *an idea is the most exciting thing there is.* Imagined melodramas about one man killing another cannot compete for enduring interest with the restructuring of the act of cognition which was Cézanne's deepest concern during the last years of his life. In one way or another, there is hardly an artist of consequence in the 20th century who was not affected by Cézanne's handling of the fundamental question "What can a man know?"

GAUGUIN—"THE RIGHT TO DARE ANYTHING"

Gauguin was a very good judge of painting, and when he had the money, between 1876 and 1880, he formed a collection of Impressionist paintings which would have got him into art history even if he himself had never touched a brush. But when he became a painter himself his instinct told him that European art needed reinvigoration and that that reinvigoration would come from sources untapped in the schools. His memories of a sojourn in Peru in childhood had convinced him that in so-called primitive art there were inherent forces that could somehow revitalize the European imagination. Working in Brittany in the 1880s, and trying to build a picture language that would be distinctly his own, he remembered the hieratic and antinaturalistic presence of the Egyptian, Assyrian, and Far Eastern sculptures which he

49. George Caleb Bingham
Fur Traders Descending the Missouri, c. 1845
The Metropolitan Museum of Art, New York

50. Peter Henry Emerson
"Taking up the Eel-Net," 1886 (platinum print)
The Museum of Modern Art, New York

Caleb Bingham's *Fur Traders Descending the Missouri (upper right)* is a famous example of the classical tradition as it expressed itself in American 19th-century painting. Whether nature came to copy art, or whether early photographers aligned themselves instinctively with art, can be debated; in any such argument, Peter Henry Emerson's photograph *"Taking up the Eel-Net" (right)* is an important piece of evidence, so closely does it parallel Bingham's austere and economical composition.

35

had seen in the Louvre. He had Japanese prints pinned up in his room, alongside reproductions of Manet's *Olympia* and paintings by Botticelli and Fra Angelico; he looked hard at the Romanesque carvings which were to be seen in Brittany near Pont-Aven. Painting his *Breton Eve* in 1889, he took her pose from a Peruvian mummy which he had seen in Paris; painting his *Yellow Christ* (fig. 51), in the same year, he took both color and pose from a polychrome wooden sculpture in the chapel at Tremalo, near Pont-Aven. By taking the statue out of the chapel and putting it in the Breton landscape he gave it, however, something specifically Gauguinesque, the sense that mysterious forces, sometimes Christian in origin and sometimes not, are at work in landscape. Where the Impressionists saw landscape as fundamentally wholesome and benign, Gauguin saw it as the henchman of the unknown, and he made us aware of this by treating the landscape, as in the *Yellow Christ,* in terms of flat bands of color that had none of the Impressionists' regard for probability. "The mysterious centers of thought" were what Gauguin wanted to reach; and with that in mind he deliberately broke with the conventions of visual experience, circumscribing the principal elements of the picture with a firm, bold line, heightening and sharpening the color, and flattening the planes until we are in no doubt that a new experience in a new kind of country is at hand.

Gauguin's personality in general was strong to the point of aggressiveness. But in one very beautiful painting done in Brittany in 1890, Gauguin subordinated his own edgy, incisive and at times almost hectoring approach to portraiture. *Marie Derrien* (pl. IX) is in fact an act of creative homage to Cézanne. More than anything that could be said or written, it shows with what a tender submission Cézanne was regarded by those of his fellow-painters who had got close to him. Gauguin gave his sitter the monumental stillness and solidity for which Cézanne strove in his own portraits. He modeled her with a sculptural fullness and firmness, building the head with rich, fat color areas. Just behind her he placed a still life by Cézanne himself. ("I cling to that picture," he once said, "as I cling to my own life.") Recreating a part of that still life on his own canvas, he went on to modulate almost imperceptibly from it to the real still life—the fruit and the tablecloth—in front of it. With a noble reticence quite foreign to his own nature, he integrated the real still life and the interpreted still life into a single, unbroken image. There was nothing of Gauguin's arbitrary, heavily-outlined handling of color; the color was Cézanne's, just as the majesty of the pose was Cézanne's. Gauguin for once did not think of himself.

Marie Derrien was an act of creative assimilation. If Gauguin's

51. Paul Gauguin
Yellow Christ, 1889
Albright-Knox Art Gallery, Buffalo, N.Y.

In the *Yellow Christ,* Gauguin drew upon the facts of the Breton countryside to project his personal vision of the Fall. Wayne Anderson remarks of the women in this painting that, "as representatives of the fallen Eve and inheritors of the stigma of original sin, they have been responsible for the suffering and death of Christ. . . ."

methods were usually more abrupt, it was because he believed that desperate situations called for desperate remedies. When he went to the South Seas it was not to "escape forever" but to save himself—and perhaps Europe too—from inanition. "A great thought-system is written in gold in Far Eastern art," he wrote in June, 1890. "The West has gone to rot, but a strong man could redouble his strength, like Antaeus, just by setting foot in the Far East. A year or two later he could come back as a new man."

Gauguin did not come back as "a new man," but the idea of the transplantable energies inherent in primitive art was to spread to Picasso, to Matisse, to Derain, to Kirchner and his colleagues in the group called Die Brücke (The Bridge) in Dresden, and to many another young artist before 1914. Gauguin saw the artist as a lord of life who could pick and choose among the past for whatever would best release his own inmost nature. In this, he pioneered one of the archetypal attitudes of the 20th century.

Gauguin also showed how color could be heightened in the interests of truth to individual human feeling; and in this, once again, his example was of primary importance to later painters. It is crucial to remember that what we call "influences" in art are not always linear. The people who profited most from Gauguin's example were not his immediate followers. Nor were they the people who tried to imitate what he had done. They were artists of quite other persuasions: Edvard Munch, most evidently, Bonnard and Vuillard in the 1890s, Picasso in his Blue Period, Matisse in 1905, Kandinsky between 1908–10. "Heighten color, simplify form" was the essence of what Gauguin told his admirers. It was Maurice Denis who said later that: "The idea of having to copy Nature had been a ball and chain for our pictorial instincts. Gauguin set us free."

What Gauguin did in the last years of the 1880s was to specify the conditions in which the artist of the future could go to work. "My own work may be only relatively good," he said later, "but I have tried to vindicate the right to dare anything." Like Nietzsche in *Beyond Good and Evil,* he wanted to get back to "the terrible original text, *Homo natura.*" "Two natures dwell within me," he wrote to his wife in 1888, "the Indian and the sensitive being. And now the sensitive being has dropped out and left the Indian to stride out ahead on his own." But the "sensitive being" in Gauguin kept coming back, unbidden, even if the Indian agreed with Nietzsche that Christian principles were "mere enfeeblement: witchcraft and sugar." But Gauguin was in touch with Paris till the end; the pictures he painted in the South Seas owed as much to Puvis de Chavannes (1824–98) and the tradition of European pastoral as to anything he picked up in Tahiti. This is

true even of paintings which, like *The Moon and the Earth* (pl. X), seem at first sight entirely non-European in their terms of reference. Gauguin did not like people to press him for a literal "explanation" of his South Seas paintings. He preferred on such occasions to quote the poet Stéphane Mallarmé: "Music needs no libretto." "The essence of a work," he wrote to one of his critics, "lies precisely in what is not expressed. . . . It has no material being."

So we may not be a great deal further forward for the knowledge that *The Moon and the Earth* represents an encounter between Hina, the moon, and Fatou, the earth. Hina stretches to her full height in order to ask Fatou if man cannot be reborn after death. When he says "No," she replies, "As you wish, but the moon will be reborn." The two figures dwarf the surrounding jungle. Gauguin has in fact given Hina the full-bodied power of one of Courbet's forest girls, while rendering the landscape in summary and miniature style, thereby reinforcing the suggestion that these are superhuman beings, personified Fates whose dialogue affects every one of us. But, once again, elements from earlier French painting keep coming in. The giant head of Fatou, for instance, is a descendant of the statues that look down on the mortals' goings-on in more than one major painting by Watteau. Degas bought this picture when it got to Paris in 1893; and as no one could have been less interested in images of the supernatural, I suspect that what he responded to was the strength and assurance with which Gauguin had reinvented the notion of pastoral.

The breakthrough which mattered to later art was the one he made in Brittany in 1888—to an abrupt, peremptory, self-willed sort of painting, in which perspective was flattened, forms were outlined with none of the continuous modeling of earlier times, and color was used with unprecedented simplicity and force.

That is what Matisse, for one, took from Gauguin: flat tones, radical contouring and the readiness to let unaccented color areas overwhelm the spectator. Bonnard and Vuillard could not have been less like pre-Columbian Peruvians, but they saw what could be made of Gauguin's arbitrary flat patterning and disregard for conventional perspective. When Gauguin used heightened color to express emotional truth, he got through to Kirchner and his colleagues in Dresden not as an "experimenter" but as a free spirit who used painting to redefine the dignity of man. We know now what Picasso meant when he said, many years later, that from a certain time onward "every man could recreate painting as he understood it from any basis whatever. . . ."

IX. Paul Gauguin
Marie Derrien, 1890
The Art Institute of Chicago

X. Paul Gauguin
The Moon and the Earth (Hina Tefatu), 1893
The Museum of Modern Art, New York

52. Vincent van Gogh
The Carpenter's Workshop, 1882
Rijksmuseum Kröller-Müller, Otterlo, Holland

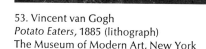

53. Vincent van Gogh
Potato Eaters, 1885 (lithograph)
The Museum of Modern Art, New York

VAN GOGH—AN APOCALYPTIC VISION

Gauguin in later years did not demur if people thought that van Gogh was fundamentally a simpleton, a Dutch dunce who had been picked up and put on the right road by him, Gauguin. Some of the facts were on his side: Gauguin knew the Impressionists when van Gogh was still toiling over his perspective-frame in The Hague, watching the workmen shambling out into their courtyards at four o'clock in the morning while the first fires were starting to smoke all over the town. In 1885–86, when Gauguin was about to make the decisive jump toward an arbitrary, inner-directed manipulation of color, van Gogh was still pondering how, in Dutch painting, "one of the most beautiful things has been the painting of *black,* which nevertheless has *light* in it." Black, which Pissarro had outlawed 20 years before!

Yet van Gogh in his Dutch years was already, even if only in intuition, the progenitor of much that is best in the art of our century. The year 1885 was, for instance, the year of the *Potato Eaters* (fig. 53), the dusky masterpiece of his years in Holland. But it was also the year in which instinct told him that color could be set free. Before he had ever seen what we call "modern painting"—that was reserved for his arrival in Paris in February, 1886—he was writing to his brother in terms that even today have kept their explosive power. Holed up in the Dutch village of Nuenen, where his father had been a pastor, he developed on his own the idea-structure which gives him so firm a hold on later art.

"*Color expresses something by itself,*" he wrote. "Let's say that I have to paint an autumn landscape with yellow leaves on the trees. If I see it as a symphony in yellow, does it matter whether the yellow that I use is the same as the yellow of the leaves? *No, it doesn't.*" So much for the ancient convention by which every object has its "local color" and must bring it everywhere as evidence of its identity.

The culmination of van Gogh's views about the moral potential of color is *The Night Café* (pl. XI), which he painted in Arles in 1888. For the Impressionists, the café was a place where people went to enjoy themselves; Degas, for one, looked at it from the standpoint of an unshakable social assurance. Van Gogh saw it quite differently: partly because it was in his nature to solidarize with the poor and the lonely, partly because he was never rich enough or assured enough to go to places where the customers did not have to count their every penny. He saw the café as "a place where one can ruin oneself, or run mad, or commit a crime." He sensed "the powers of darkness" in what was probably a straightforward French working-class drink shop; and he tried, when painting it, "to express the terrible passions of humanity by means of red and green." His account of the painting is explicit enough to deserve quotation. The room, he said, was "blood red and dark yellow, with a green billiard table in the middle." Four lemon yellow lamps cast a glow of orange and green. The blood red and the yellow and the sharp green of the billiard cloth contrasted with "the tender, soft, Louis XV green of the counter, with its pink bouquet of cut flowers." The atmosphere was full—or so it seemed to van Gogh—of pale sulphur, "like a devil's furnace"; and the owner's white coat was changed to "lemon yellow, or a pale, luminous green" as he stood on duty in the corner.

Now, it is quite clear from a painting which Gauguin made of this same café that van Gogh misrepresented its basic nature, which was that of a place where people sat not too far apart and stared boldly around them. Van Gogh's inner distresses caused him to present the café as a place where a few cheerless patrons were swept to the perimeter of the scene, the way snow is swept into the gutters of a roadway. All possibility of an amiable human intercourse seems excluded, and we genuinely feel, as he wished us to feel, that "the terrible passions of humanity" have run their course behind the half-drawn curtain at the back of the room. Even the billiard table, that robust old stand-in for a more active and constructive way of life, suddenly looks like a bier. Van Gogh achieves all this in part by manipulations of perspective; but it is above all the color that projects a sense of the most penetrating inner anguish. Truth to feeling had never come out more strongly in painting. By setting truth to individual feeling above truth to objective fact, van Gogh gave the colorist his charter. Those words of his in 1885 are the beginnings of much of Matisse, much of Munch, much of early Derain and Vlaminck, much of Kandinsky, much of Chagall in his early years, much of Klee. To this day, when artists talk about color, they owe something, directly or indirectly, to van Gogh.

Van Gogh was also coming to terms at that time with what is for the layman one of the most bothersome aspects of modern art: distortion. Distortion is, or was, a sore subject with young and old alike. We remember, for instance, how in 1913 the art students of Chicago burned Matisse's *Blue Nude* in effigy when it came to the city as part of the Armory Show. And it was an "artist" who complained to van Gogh's brother about the distortions in the *Potato Eaters*. "Tell him," van Gogh wrote, "that I should be in despair if my figures were 'correct,' in academic terms. I don't want them to be 'correct.' Real artists paint things not as they are, in a dry, analytical way, but as *they* feel them. Tell him that I adore Michelangelo's figures, though the legs are too long and the hips and backsides too large. Tell him that what I most want to do is to make of these incorrectnesses, deviations, remodelings or adjustments of reality something that is—yes, 'untrue,' if you like, but more true than literal truth."

This was, once again, written in the year 1885, and in the

54. Vincent van Gogh
Street in Les Saintes-Maries, 1888
The Museum of Modern Art, New York

55. Vincent van Gogh
Stairway at Auvers, 1890
The St. Louis Art Museum

XI. Vincent van Gogh
The Night Café, 1888
Yale University Art Gallery, New Haven, Conn.

XII. Vincent van Gogh
The Starry Night, 1889
The Museum of Modern Art, New York

56. Vincent van Gogh
Hospital Corridor at Saint-Rémy, 1889–1890
The Museum of Modern Art, New York

depths of the Dutch countryside. Again van Gogh hit on just the turn of phrase that could stand as a motto for the century that is now three-quarters over. To "paint things not as they are ... but as *they* feel them" is an ambition so nearly universal in our time that van Gogh would deserve immortality for that phrase alone. Yet he went on finding, to the end of his short life, the right words for the kind of work which would bring to light the buried life of man. Before how many great paintings of this century do we not remember van Gogh saying that "the painter of the future will be a colorist such as there has never been," and that the unit of expression for the new art would be "a form of brushwork that would cut out stippling, and the rest, and offer simply the varied stroke"?

In pictures like *The Starry Night* (pl. XII), painted in Saint-Rémy in June, 1889, van Gogh showed what he meant. The paint in *The Starry Night* is not applied in polite, well-judged, art school style. It forms itself into ideograms of convulsion: emblems of an apocalyptic vision which includes stars brighter than the sun at midday, a huge horned moon that seems to hold the sun in its embrace, and a spiral nebula that flies through the air like a serpent from the Book of Revelations. Even the moonlit woodlands behind the little town are rendered with a ferocious, nonstop, over-and-over movement of the loaded brush. Just once or twice before, others had got somewhere near to the intensity of *The Starry Night*: Leonardo da Vinci in his drawings of a storm, the German Old Master Altdorfer in his portrayals of a tormented northern sky; but van Gogh was out on his own for the sheer visionary intensity of his new "unit of expression." This is painting that refers not to earlier painting but to areas of our experience to which painting had not previously had access.

To Cézanne's "What can a man know?" van Gogh added a question of his own: "How can we best unlock the valves of feeling?" To one or the other of these questions, or to both of them in conjunction, modern art has the answers.

SUGGESTED READINGS

General

Arnason, H. H. *History of Modern Art.*
New York, Abrams, 1968.

Clark, Kenneth. *Civilisation: A Personal View.*
New York and Evanston, Harper and Row, 1970.

Gaunt, William. *Impressionism: A Visual History with 108 Plates in Full Color.*
New York, Praeger; London, Thames and Hudson, 1970.

Gombrich, E. H. *The Story of Art.*
London, Phaidon, 1972.

Hamilton, George Heard. *19th and 20th Century Art.*
New York, Abrams, 1970.

Holt, Elizabeth Gilmore, ed. *From the Classicists to the Impressionists:*
A Documentary History of Art and Architecture in the Nineteenth Century.
Garden City, N.Y., Doubleday, 1966.

Jaffé, Hans L. C. *The World of the Impressionists.*
Maplewood, N.J., Hammond, 1969.

Pool, Phoebe. *Impressionism.*
New York, Praeger, 1967.

Read, Herbert. *A Concise History of Modern Painting.* Rev. ed.
New York, Praeger, 1969.

Rewald, John. *The History of Impressionism.* 4th rev. ed.
New York, The Museum of Modern Art, 1973.

Rewald, John. *Post-Impressionism: From van Gogh to Gauguin.* Rev. ed.
New York, The Museum of Modern Art, 1962.

Paul Cézanne

Andersen, Wayne. *Cézanne's Portrait Drawings.*
Cambridge, Mass., MIT Press, 1970.

Fry, Roger. *Cézanne: A Study of His Development.* 6th rev. ed.
First publ. in 1927.
New York, Noonday Press, 1970.

Huyghe, René. *Cézanne.*
New York, Abrams, 1959.

Lindsay, Jack. *Cézanne: His Life and Art.*
Greenwich, Conn., New York Graphic Society, 1969.

Murphy, Richard W. *The World of Cézanne, 1839–1906.*
(Time-Life Library of Art).
New York, Time-Life, 1968.

Schapiro, Meyer. *Paul Cézanne.* (Library of Great Painters ser.).
New York, Abrams, 1969.

Tyler, Parker. *Cézanne, Gauguin.* (World Art ser.).
Garden City, N.Y., Doubleday, 1969.

Paul Gauguin

Andersen, Wayne. *Gauguin's Paradise Lost.*
New York, Viking, 1971.

Goldwater, Robert. *Paul Gauguin.* (Library of Great Painters ser.).
New York, Abrams, 1957.

Jaworska, Wladyslawa. *Gauguin and the Pont-Aven School.*
Greenwich, Conn., New York Graphic Society, 1972.

Rewald, John. *Paul Gauguin.* (Portfolio ser.).
New York, Abrams, 1969.

Russell, John. *Gauguin.*
Lausanne, UNESCO and Editions Rencontre, 1970.

Werner, Alfred. *Paul Gauguin.*
New York, McGraw-Hill, 1967.

Vincent van Gogh

Barr, Alfred H., Jr. and Brooks, Charles M., Jr. *Vincent van Gogh: A Monograph.*
Reprint 1942 ed.
New York, Arno for The Museum of Modern Art, 1967.

Cabanne, Pierre. *Van Gogh.*
New York, Abrams, 1971.

Gogh, Vincent van. *The Complete Letters of Vincent van Gogh.* Limited ed.
Greenwich, Conn., New York Graphic Society, 1958.

Keller, Horst. *Van Gogh: The Final Years.*
New York, Abrams, 1970.

Hammacher, A. M. *Genius and Disaster: The Ten Creative Years of Van Gogh.*
New York, Abrams, 1968.

La Faille, J. B. de. *The Works of Vincent van Gogh: His Paintings and Drawings.*
Rev. and enl. ed.
New York, Reynal, 1970.

Roskill, Mark. *Van Gogh, Gauguin and the Impressionist Circle.*
Greenwich, Conn., New York Graphic Society, 1970.

Wallace, Robert. *World of Van Gogh.* (Time-Life Library of Art).
New York, Time-Life, 1969

Georges Seurat

Courthion, Pierre. *Georges Seurat.*
New York, Abrams, 1968.

Rewald, John. *Georges Seurat.*
New York, Wittenborn, 1943.

Russell, John. *Seurat.* (World of Art ser.).
London, Thames and Hudson; New York, Praeger, 1965.

LIST OF ILLUSTRATIONS

Dimensions: height precedes width; a third dimension, depth, is given for sculptures and constructions where relevant. Foreign titles are in English, except in cases where the title does not translate or is better known in its original form. Asterisked titles indicate works reproduced in color.

Anthony, Edward
(1818–88)

Broadway on a Rainy Day, 1859 (fig. 21)
Stereograph
George Eastman House, Rochester, N.Y.

Bingham, George Caleb
(1811–79)

Fur Traders Descending the Missouri, c. 1845
    (fig. 49)
Oil on canvas, 29 x 36½ inches
The Metropolitan Museum of Art, New York
Morris K. Jesup Fund, 1933

Bonnard, Pierre
(1867–1947)

Screen, 1897 (fig. 28)
Lithograph in four panels, each 53¼ x 17¾
    inches (sight)
The Museum of Modern Art, New York
Abby Aldrich Rockefeller Purchase Fund

Capa, Robert
(1913–54)

"Collaborationist," Chartres, France, 1944 (fig. 25)
Photograph
The Museum of Modern Art, New York
Gift of Cornell Capa

Cézanne, Paul
(1839–1906)

Portrait of Camille Pissarro, c. 1873 (fig. 40)
Pencil, 3⅞ x 3⅛ inches
Mr. and Mrs. John Rewald, New York

The Card Players, 1890–92 (fig. 45)
Oil on canvas, 25½ x 32 inches
The Metropolitan Museum of Art, New York
Bequest of Stephen C. Clark, 1960

Still Life with Peppermint Bottle (pl. VII)
Oil on canvas, 26 x 32⅜ inches
National Gallery of Art, Washington, D.C.
Chester Dale Collection

Still Life with Apples, 1895–98 (fig. 42)
Oil on canvas, 27 x 36½ inches
The Museum of Modern Art, New York
Lillie P. Bliss Collection

Mont Ste. Victoire Seen from Bibemus Quarry,
    c. 1898–1900 (fig. 43)
Oil on canvas, 25½ x 32 inches
The Baltimore Museum of Art
Cone Collection

Grandes Baigneuses, 1898–1905 (pl. VIII)
Oil on canvas, 82 x 99 inches
Philadelphia Museum of Art
W. P. Wilstach Collection

Le Château Noir, 1904–06 (fig. 46)
Oil on canvas, 29 x 36¾ inches
The Museum of Modern Art, New York
Gift of Mrs. David M. Levy

Chéret, Jules
(1836–1933)

Les Girard, L'Horloge, Champs-Elysées, 1879
    (fig. 36)
Lithograph, 22⅝ x 17 inches
The Museum of Modern Art, New York
Acquired by exchange

Corot, Jean Baptiste Camille
(1796–1875)

Breton Women at a Well, 1850–55 (fig. 48)
Oil on canvas, 7 x 9½ inches
Musée du Louvre, Paris

Courbet, Gustave
(1819–77)

The Trellis, 1863 (fig. 11)
Oil on canvas, 43¼ x 53¼ inches
The Toledo Museum of Art, Toledo, Ohio
Gift of Edward Drummond Libbey

David, Jacques Louis
(1748–1825)

Marat Assassinated, 1793 (fig. 2)
Oil on canvas, 63¾ x 49¼ inches
Musées Royaux des Beaux-Arts de Belgique,
    Brussels

Degas, Edgar
(1834–1917)

Degas seated, with sculpture in the background
    (fig. 23)
Photograph
The Metropolitan Museum of Art, New York
Gift of Mrs. Henry T. Curtiss, 1964

Café Singer Wearing a Glove, 1878 (pl. III)
Pastel and tempera, 20⅞ x 16⅛ inches
Fogg Art Museum, Harvard University,
    Cambridge, Mass.
Bequest The Collection of Maurice Wertheim

Eakins, Thomas
(1844–1916)

Portrait of Miss Amelia van Buren, 1889–91
    (fig. 30)
Oil on canvas, 45 x 32 inches
The Phillips Collection, Washington, D.C.

Miss Amelia van Buren, c. 1891 (fig. 29)
Photograph
Philadelphia Museum of Art
Given by Mr. Seymour Adelman

Emerson, Peter Henry
(1856–1936)

"Taking up the Eel-Net"
    from *Life and Landscape on the Norfolk
    Broads* by P. H. Emerson and T. F. Goodall,
    1886 (fig. 50)
Platinum print
The Museum of Modern Art, New York
Gift of William A. Grigsby

Gance, Abel
(b. 1889)

Antonin Artaud as Marat, in a scene
    from *Napoléon,* 1926 (fig. 24)
Film still
The Museum of Modern Art, New York
Film Stills Archive

Gauguin, Paul
(1848–1903)

Yellow Christ, 1889 (fig. 51)
Oil on canvas, 36¼ x 28⅞ inches
Albright-Knox Art Gallery, Buffalo, N.Y.

Self-Portrait with Halo, 1889 (fig. 31)
Oil on wood, 31¼ x 20¼ inches
National Gallery of Art, Washington, D.C.
Chester Dale Collection

*Marie Derrien, 1890 (pl. IX)
Oil on canvas, 25⅝ x 21½ inches
The Art Institute of Chicago
The Joseph Winterbotham Collection

*The Moon and the Earth (Hina Tefatu), 1893 (pl. X)
Oil on burlap, 45 x 24½ inches
The Museum of Modern Art, New York
Lillie P. Bliss Collection

*Whence do we come? What are we? Where are
    we going?* 1897 (fig. 33)
Oil on canvas, 4 feet 5¾ inches x 12 feet
    3½ inches
Museum of Fine Arts, Boston
Arthur Gordon Tompkins Residuary Fund

Géricault, Théodore
(1791–1824)

The Raft of the "Méduse," 1818–19 (fig. 4)
Oil on canvas, 16 feet 1⅜ inches x 23 feet
    6⅛ inches
Musée du Louvre, Paris

Gogh, Vincent van
(1853–90)

The Carpenter's Workshop, 1882 (fig. 52)
Pencil and watercolor, 11 x 18½ inches
Rijksmuseum Kröller-Müller, Otterlo, Holland

Potato Eaters, 1885 (fig. 53)
Lithograph, 12¼ x 15¾ inches
The Museum of Modern Art, New York
Gift of Mr. and Mrs. A. A. Rosen

Self-Portrait, 1888 (fig. 32)
Oil on canvas, 24½ x 20½ inches
Fogg Art Museum, Harvard University,
    Cambridge, Mass.
Bequest The Collection of Maurice Wertheim

Street in Les Saintes-Maries, 1888 (fig. 54)
Ink and reed pen, 9⅝ x 12½ inches
The Museum of Modern Art, New York
Abby Aldrich Rockefeller Bequest

*The Night Café, 1888 (pl. XI)
Oil on canvas, 28½ x 36¼ inches
Yale University Art Gallery, New Haven, Conn.
Bequest of Stephen Carlton Clark, B.A., 1903

*The Starry Night, 1889 (pl. XII)
Oil on canvas, 29 x 36¼ inches
The Museum of Modern Art, New York
Acquired through the Lillie P. Bliss Bequest

Hospital Corridor at Saint-Rémy, 1889–90 (fig. 56)
Gouache and watercolor, 24⅛ x 18⅝ inches
The Museum of Modern Art, New York
Abby Aldrich Rockefeller Bequest

Stairway at Auvers, 1890 (fig. 55)
Oil on canvas, 20 x 30 inches
The St. Louis Art Museum

Le Nain, Louis
(c. 1593–1648)

Peasants in a Landscape, c. 1641 (fig. 47)
Oil on canvas, 16⅜ x 21¾ inches
Wadsworth Atheneum, Hartford, Conn.
The Ella Gallup Sumner and Mary Catlin Collection

Manet, Edouard
(1832–83)

Le Déjeuner sur l'herbe, 1863 (fig. 13)
Oil on canvas, 6 feet 10 inches x 8 feet 8¼ inches
Musée du Louvre, Paris

Olympia, 1863 (fig. 10)
Oil on canvas, 51⅜ x 74¾ inches
Musée du Louvre, Paris

Portrait of Emile Zola, 1868 (fig. 14)
Oil on canvas, 57⅝ x 44⅞ inches
Musée du Louvre, Paris

*The Folkestone Boat, Boulogne, 1869 (pl. I)
Oil on canvas, 23½ x 28⅞ inches
Philadelphia Museum of Art
Mr. and Mrs. Carroll S. Tyson Collection

Menzel, Adolf von
(1815–1905)

*The Departure of Kaiser Wilhelm from Berlin on
    July 31, 1870, to Join the Troops at the Front*
    (fig. 19)
Oil on canvas, 25¼ x 31¼ inches
Nationalgalerie, Berlin

Monet, Claude
(1840–1926)

Bazille and Camille, c. 1865 (fig. 15)
Oil on canvas, 36⅝ x 27⅛ inches
National Gallery of Art, Washington, D.C.
Ailsa Mellon Bruce Collection

The River, 1868 (fig. 16)
Oil on canvas, 31⅞ x 39½ inches
The Art Institute of Chicago
The Potter Palmer Collection

*The Gare Saint-Lazare, Paris, 1877 (pl. II)
Oil on canvas, 32½ x 39¾ inches
Fogg Art Museum, Harvard University,
    Cambridge, Mass.
Bequest The Collection of Maurice Wertheim

Munch, Edvard
(1863–1944)

The Shriek, 1896 (fig. 8)
Lithograph, 20⅝ x 15¾ inches
The Museum of Modern Art, New York
Matthew T. Mellon Fund

August Strindberg, 1896 (fig. 17)
Lithograph, 19⅞ x 14⅞ inches
The Museum of Modern Art, New York
Abby Aldrich Rockefeller Fund

Henrik Ibsen in the Grand Café, Christiania, 1902
    (fig. 18)
Lithograph, 16¾ x 23¼ inches
Munch-museet, Oslo

47

Partridge, Rondal

El Camino Real, Palo Alto, California
    from *God's Own Junkyard* by Peter Blake,
    published Holt, Rinehart and Winston,
    New York, 1964 (fig. 22)
Photograph
Courtesy of the photographer

Penfield, Edward
(1866–1925)

Harper's March, 1897 (fig. 27)
Poster, 18⅞ x 13⅞ inches
The Museum of Modern Art, New York
Gift of Mr. and Mrs. Leo Farland

Penn, Irving
(b. 1917)

Colette, Paris, 1951
    from *Moments Preserved: Eight Essays in
    Photographs and Words* by Irving Penn,
    published Simon & Schuster, New York, 1960
    (fig. 26)
Photograph
The Museum of Modern Art, New York
Gift of the photographer, 1958
(Copyright © by The Condé Nast Publications
    Inc.)

Picasso, Pablo
(1881–1973)

The Charnel House, 1945 (fig. 9)
Oil and charcoal on canvas, 78⅝ x 98½ inches
The Museum of Modern Art, New York
Mrs. Sam A. Lewisohn Bequest (by exchange) and
    Purchase

Pissarro, Camille
(1831–1903)

Jallais Hill, Pontoise, 1867 (fig. 20)
Oil on canvas, 34¼ x 45¼ inches
The Metropolitan Museum of Art, New York
Bequest of William Church Osborn, 1951

The River Oise near Pontoise, 1873 (fig. 34)
Oil on canvas, 18 x 21¾ inches
Sterling and Francine Clark Art Institute,
    Williamstown, Mass.

Portrait of Cézanne, 1874 (fig. 41)
Etching, 10⅝ x 8½ inches
S. P. Avery Collection, Prints Division,
The New York Public Library, Astor, Lenox and
    Tilden Foundations

* *The Climbing Path at the Hermitage, Pontoise,*
    1875 (pl. V)
Oil on canvas, 24½ x 25¾ inches
The Brooklyn Museum
Gift of Dirkan G. Kelekian

Poussin, Nicolas
(1593/4–1665)

Massacre of the Innocents (detail), 1630–31 (fig. 7)
Oil on canvas, 57⅞ x 67⅜ inches
Musée Condé, Chantilly

Landscape with St. John at Patmos, 1645–50
    (fig. 44)
Oil on canvas, 40 x 52¼ inches
The Art Institute of Chicago
The A. A. Munger Collection

Rembrandt van Ryn
(1606–69)

The Jewish Bride (Isaac and Rebecca?) (fig. 6)
Oil on canvas, 48 x 66 inches
Rijksmuseum, Amsterdam

Renoir, Pierre Auguste
(1841–1919)

Monet Painting in His Garden at Argenteuil, 1873
    (fig. 12)
Oil on canvas, 18⅜ x 23½ inches
Wadsworth Atheneum, Hartford, Conn.
Bequest of Anne Parrish Titzell

* *The Luncheon of the Boating Party,* 1881 (pl. IV)
Oil on canvas, 51⅜ x 69¼ inches
The Phillips Collection, Washington, D.C.

Saint-Aubin, Gabriel-Jacques de
(1724–80)

A Street Show in Paris (La Parade du boulevard)
    (fig. 38)
Oil on canvas, 31½ x 25¼ inches
The National Gallery, London

Seurat, Georges
(1859–91)

Place de la Concorde, Winter, 1882–83 (fig. 39)
Conté crayon and chalk, 9⅛ x 12⅛ inches
The Solomon R. Guggenheim Museum, New York

*Sunday Afternoon on the Island of La Grande
    Jatte,* 1884–86 (fig. 37)
Oil on canvas, 6 feet 9 inches x 10 feet
The Art Institute of Chicago
Helen Birch Bartlett Memorial Collection

* *Invitation to the Side-Show (La Parade),* 1887–88
    (pl. VI)
Oil on canvas, 39¼ x 59 inches
The Metropolitan Museum of Art, New York
Bequest of Stephen C. Clark, 1961

Le Chahut, 1890 (fig. 35)
Oil on canvas, 67⅛ x 55¼ inches
Rijksmuseum Kröller-Müller, Otterlo, Holland

Turner, J. M. W.
(1775–1851)

Burning of the Houses of Parliament, 1834 (fig. 3)
Oil on canvas, 36½ x 48½ inches
The Cleveland Museum of Art
Bequest of John L. Severance

Velázquez, Diego Rodriguez de Silva
(1599–1660)

The Surrender of Breda, 1634–35 (fig. 1)
Oil on canvas, 10 feet x 12 feet
Museo Nacional del Prado, Madrid

Wright of Derby, Joseph
(1734–97)

The Old Man and Death, c. 1774 (fig. 5)
Oil on canvas, 40 x 50 inches
Wadsworth Atheneum, Hartford, Conn.